SELECTED POEMS

1923-1958

by the same author

73 poems

e.e. cummings

---

selected poems
1923-1958

faber and faber
LONDON · BOSTON

First published in 1960
by Faber and Faber Limited
3 Queen Square London WC1N 3AU
First published in this edition in 1969

Printed in England by Clays Ltd, St Ives plc
All rights reserved

A CIP record for this book is available
from the British Library

ISBN 0 571 08986 0

12 14 16 18 20 19 17 15 13 11

this selection has been made by the author from eleven books of poems; ten of them constituting a volume called *Poems 1923–1954*, while the eleventh (published in 1958) is entitled *95 Poems*

in Just-
spring   when the world is mud-
luscious the little
lame balloonman

whistles   far   and wee

and eddieandbill come
running from marbles and
piracies and it's
spring

when the world is puddle-wonderful

the queer
old balloonman whistles
far   and   wee
and bettyandisbel come dancing

from hop-scotch and jump-rope and

it's
spring
and
        the

            goat-footed

balloonMan   whistles
far
and
wee

my love
thy hair is one kingdom
　　the king whereof is darkness
thy forehead is a flight of flowers

thy head is a quick forest
　　filled with sleeping birds
thy breasts are swarms of white bees
　　upon the bough of thy body
thy body to me is April
in whose armpits is the approach of spring

thy thighs are white horses yoked to a chariot
　　of kings
they are the striking of a good minstrel
between them is always a pleasant song

my love
thy head is a casket
　　of the cool jewel of thy mind
the hair of thy head is one warrior
　　innocent of defeat
thy hair upon thy shoulders is·an army
　　with victory and with trumpets

thy legs are the trees of dreaming
whose fruit is the very eatage of forgetfulness

thy lips are satraps in scarlet
　　in whose kiss is the combining of kings
thy wrists
are holy
　　which are the keepers of the keys of thy blood
thy feet upon thy ankles are flowers in vases
　　of silver

in thy beauty is the dilemma of flutes

thy eyes are the betrayal
of bells comprehended through incense

O sweet spontaneous
earth how often have
the
doting

     fingers of
prurient philosophers pinched
and
poked

thee
, has the naughty thumb
of science prodded
thy

   beauty   . how
often have religions taken
thee upon their scraggy knees
squeezing and

buffeting thee that thou mightest conceive
gods
    (but
true

to the incomparable
couch of death thy
rhythmic
lover

    thou answerest

them only with

      spring)

Buffalo Bill's
defunct
          who used to
          ride a watersmooth-silver
                                        stallion
and break onetwothreefourfive pigeonsjustlikethat
                                                        Jesus

he was a handsome man
                         and what i want to know is
how do you like your blueeyed boy
Mister Death

it may not always be so; and i say
that if your lips, which i have loved, should touch
another's, and your dear strong fingers clutch
his heart, as mine in time not far away;
if on another's face your sweet hair lay
in such a silence as i know, or such
great writhing words as, uttering overmuch,
stand helplessly before the spirit at bay;

if this should be, i say if this should be—
you of my heart, send me a little word;
that i may go unto him, and take his hands,
saying, Accept all happiness from me.
Then shall i turn my face, and hear one bird
sing terribly afar in the lost lands.

suppose
Life is an old man carrying flowers on his head.

young death sits in a café
smiling, a piece of money held between
his thumb and first finger

(i say "will he buy flowers" to you
and "Death is young
life wears velour trousers
life totters, life has a beard" i

say to you who are silent.—"Do you see
Life? he is there and here,
or that, or this
or nothing or an old man 3 thirds
asleep, on his head
flowers, always crying
to nobody something about les
roses les bluets
        yes,
          will He buy?
Les belles bottes—oh hear
, pas chères")

and my love slowly answered I think so.   But
I think I see someone else

there is a lady, whose name is Afterwards
she is sitting beside young death, is slender;
likes flowers.

Spring is like a perhaps hand
(which comes carefully
out of Nowhere)arranging
a window,into which people look(while
people stare
arranging and changing placing
carefully there a strange
thing and a known thing here)and

changing everything carefully

spring is like a perhaps
Hand in a window
(carefully to
and fro moving New and
Old things,while
people stare carefully
moving a perhaps
fraction of flower here placing
an inch of air there)and

without breaking anything.

who knows if the moon's
a balloon,coming out of a keen city
in the sky—filled with pretty people?
(and if you and i should

get into it,if they
should take me and take you into their balloon,
why then
we'd go up higher with all the pretty people

than houses and steeples and clouds:
go sailing
away and away sailing into a keen
city which nobody's ever visited,where

always
          it's
                    Spring)and everyone's
in love and flowers pick themselves

i like my body when it is with your
body.   It is so quite new a thing.
Muscles better and nerves more.
i like your body.   i like what it does,
i like its hows.   i like to feel the spine
of your body and its bones, and the trembling
-firm-smooth ness and which i will
again and again and again
kiss, i like kissing this and that of you,
i like, slowly stroking the, shocking fuzz
of your electric fur, and what-is-it comes
over parting flesh . . . . And eyes big love-crumbs,

and possibly i like the thrill

of under me you so quite new

little tree
little silent Christmas tree
you are so little
you are more like a flower

who found you in the green forest
and were you very sorry to come away?
see   i will comfort you
because you smell so sweetly

i will kiss your cool bark
and hug you safe and tight
just as your mother would,
only don't be afraid

look   the spangles
that sleep all the year in a dark box
dreaming of being taken out and allowed to shine,
the balls the chains red and gold the fluffy threads,

put up your little arms
and i'll give them all to you to hold
every finger shall have its ring
and there won't be a single place dark or unhappy

then when you're quite dressed
you'll stand in the window for everyone to see
and how they'll stare!
oh but you'll be very proud

and my little sister and i will take hands
and looking up at our beautiful tree
we'll dance and sing
"Noel Noel"

Humanity i love you
because you would rather black the boots of
success than enquire whose soul dangles from his
watch-chain which would be embarrassing for both

parties and because you
unflinchingly applaud all
songs containing the words country home and
mother when sung at the old howard

Humanity i love you because
when you're hard up you pawn your
intelligence to buy a drink and when
you're flush pride keeps

you from the pawn shop and
because you are continually committing
nuisances but more
especially in your own house

Humanity i love you because you
are perpetually putting the secret of
life in your pants and forgetting
it's there and sitting down

on it
and because you are
forever making poems in the lap
of death Humanity

i hate you

POEM, OR BEAUTY HURTS MR. VINAL

take it from me kiddo
believe me
my country, 'tis of

you, land of the Cluett
Shirt Boston Garter and Spearmint
Girl With The Wrigley Eyes (of you
land of the Arrow Ide
and Earl &
Wilson
Collars) of you i
sing: land of Abraham Lincoln and Lydia E. Pinkham,
land above all of Just Add Hot Water And Serve—
from every B. V. D.

let freedom ring

amen.   i do however protest, anent the un
-spontaneous and otherwise scented merde which
greets one (Everywhere Why) as divine poesy per
that and this radically defunct periodical.   i would

suggest that certain ideas gestures
rhymes, like Gillette Razor Blades
having been used and reused
to the mystical moment of dullness emphatically are
Not To Be Resharpened.   (Case in point

if we are to believe these gently O sweetly
melancholy trillers amid the thrillers
these crepuscular violinists among my and your
skyscrapers— Helen & Cleopatra were Just Too Lovely,
The Snail's On The Thorn enter Morn and God's
In His andsoforth

do you get me?) according
to such supposedly indigenous
throstles Art is O World O Life
a formula: example, Turn Your Shirttails Into
Drawers and If It Isn't An Eastman It Isn't A
Kodak therefore my friends let
us now sing each and all fortissimo A-
mer
i

ca, I
love,
You.   And there're a
hun-dred-mil-lion-oth-ers, like
all of you successfully if
delicately gelded (or spaded)
gentlemen (and ladies)— pretty

littleliverpill-
hearted-Nujolneeding-There's-A-Reason
americans (who tensetendoned and with
upward vacant eyes, painfully
perpetually crouched, quivering, upon the
sternly allotted sandpile
—how silently
emit a tiny violetflavoured nuisance: Odor?

ono.
comes out like a ribbon lies flat on the brush

nobody loses all the time

i had an uncle named
Sol who was a born failure and
nearly everybody said he should have gone
into vaudeville perhaps because my Uncle Sol could
sing McCann He Was A Diver on Xmas Eve like Hell Itself which
may or may not account for the fact that my Uncle

Sol indulged in that possibly most inexcusable
of all to use a highfalootin phrase
luxuries that is or to
wit farming and be
it needlessly
added

my Uncle Sol's farm
failed because the chickens
ate the vegetables so
my Uncle Sol had a
chicken farm till the
skunks ate the chickens when

my Uncle Sol
had a skunk farm but
the skunks caught cold and
died and so
my Uncle Sol imitated the
skunks in a subtle manner

or by drowning himself in the watertank
but somebody who'd given my Uncle Sol a Victor
Victrola and records while he lived presented to
him upon the auspicious occasion of his decease a
scrumptious not to mention splendiferous funeral with
tall boys in black gloves and flowers and everything and

i remember we all cried like the Missouri
when my Uncle Sol's coffin lurched because
somebody pressed a button
(and down went
my Uncle
Sol

and started a worm farm)

mr youse needn't be so spry
concernin questions arty

each has his tastes but as for i
i likes a certain party

gimme the he-man's solid bliss
for youse ideas i'll match youse

a pretty girl who naked is
is worth a million statues

she being Brand

-new;and you
know consequently a
little stiff i was
careful of her and(having

thoroughly oiled the universal
joint tested my gas felt of
her radiator made sure her springs were O.

K.)i went right to it flooded-the-carburetor cranked her

up,slipped the
clutch(and then somehow got into reverse she
kicked what
the hell)next
minute i was back in neutral tried and

again slo-wly;bare,ly nudg.   ing(my

lev-er Right-
oh and her gears being in
A 1 shape passed
from low through
second-in-to-high like
greasedlightning)just as we turned the corner of Divinity

avenue i touched the accelerator and give

her the juice,good

                    (it
was the first ride and believe i we was
happy to see how nice she acted right up to
the last minute coming back down by the Public
Gardens i slammed on
the

internalexpanding
&
externalcontracting
brakes Bothatonce and

brought allof her tremB
-ling
to a:dead.

stand-
;Still)

MEMORABILIA

stop look &

listen Venezia: incline thine
ear you glassworks
of Murano;
pause
elevator nel
mezzo del cammin' that means half-
way up the Campanile, believe

thou me cocodrillo—

mine eyes have seen
the glory of

the coming of
the Americans particularly the
brand of marriageable nymph which is
armed with large legs rancid
voices Baedekers Mothers and kodaks
—by night upon the Riva Schiavoni or in
the felicitous vicinity of the de l'Europe

Grand and Royal
Danielli their numbers

are like unto the stars of Heaven. . . .

i do signore
affirm that all gondola signore
day below me gondola signore gondola
and above me pass loudly and gondola
rapidly denizens of Omaha Altoona or what
not enthusiastic cohorts from Duluth God only,
gondola knows Cincingondolanati i gondola don't

—the substantial dollarbringing virgins

"from the Loggia where
are we angels by O yes
beautiful we now pass through the look
girls in the style of that's the
foliage what is it didn't Ruskin
says about you got the haven't Marjorie
isn't this wellcurb simply darling"
                                        —O Education:O

thos cook & son

(O to be a metope
now that triglyph's here)

a man who had fallen among thieves
lay by the roadside on his back
dressed in fifteenthrate ideas
wearing a round jeer for a hat

fate per a somewhat more than less
emancipated evening
had in return for consciousness
endowed him with a changeless grin

whereon a dozen staunch and leal
citizens did graze at pause
then fired by hypercivic zeal
sought newer pastures or because

swaddled with a frozen brook
of pinkest vomit out of eyes
which noticed nobody he looked
as if he did not care to rise

one hand did nothing on the vest
its wideflung friend clenched weakly dirt
while the mute trouserfly confessed
a button solemnly inert.

Brushing from whom the stiffened puke
i put him all into my arms
and staggered banged with terror through
a million billion trillion stars

voices to voices, lip to lip
i swear (to noone everyone) constitutes
undying; or whatever this and that petal confutes . . .
to exist being a peculiar form of sleep

what's beyond logic happens beneath will;
nor can these moments be translated: i say
that even after April
by God there is no excuse for May

—bring forth your flowers and machinery: sculpture and prose
flowers guess and miss
machinery is the more accurate, yes
it delivers the goods, Heaven knows

(yet are we mindful, though not as yet awake,
of ourselves which shout and cling, being
for a little while and which easily break
in spite of the best overseeing)

i mean that the blond absence of any program.
except last and always and first to live
makes unimportant what i and you believe;
nor for philosophy does this rose give a damn . . .

bring on your fireworks, which are a mixed
splendor of piston and of pistil; very well
provided an instant may be fixed
so that it will not rub, like any other pastel.

(While you and i have lips and voices which
are for kissing and to sing with
who cares if some oneeyed son of a bitch
invents an instrument to measure Spring with?

each dream nascitur, is not made . . .)
why then to Hell with that: the other; this,
since the thing perhaps is
to eat flowers and not to be afraid.

"next to of course god america i
love you land of the pilgrims' and so forth oh
say can you see by the dawn's early my
country 'tis of centuries come and go
and are no more what of it we should worry
in every language even deafanddumb
thy sons acclaim your glorious name by gorry
by jingo by gee by gosh by gum
why talk of beauty what could be more beautiful than these heroic happy dead
who rushed like lions to the roaring slaughter
they did not stop to think they died instead
then shall the voice of liberty be mute?"

He spoke.   And drank rapidly a glass of water

my sweet old etcetera
aunt lucy during the recent

war could and what
is more did tell you just
what everybody was fighting

for,
my   sister

isabel created hundreds
(and
hundreds)of socks not to
mention shirts fleaproof earwarmers

etcetera wristers etcetera, my
mother hoped that

i would die etcetera
bravely of course my father used
to become hoarse talking about how it was
a privilege and if only he
could meanwhile my

self etcetera lay quietly
in the deep mud et

cetera
(dreaming,
et
    cetera, of
Your smile
eyes knees and of your Etcetera)

here's a little mouse)and
what does he think about, i
wonder as over this
floor(quietly with

bright eyes)drifts(nobody
can tell because
Nobody knows, or why
jerks Here &, here,
gr(oo)ving the room's Silence)this like
a littlest
poem a
(with wee ears and see?

tail frisks)
                    (gonE)
"mouse",
              We are not the same you and

i, since here's a little he
or is
it It
?   (or was something we saw in the mirror)?

therefore we'll kiss; for maybe
what was Disappeared
into ourselves
who   (look).   ,startled

in spite of everything
which breathes and moves, since Doom
(with white longest hands
neatening each crease)
will smooth entirely our minds

—before leaving my room
i turn, and(stooping
through the morning)kiss
this pillow, dear
where our heads lived and were.

since feeling is first
who pays any attention
to the syntax of things
will never wholly kiss you;

wholly to be a fool
while Spring is in the world

my blood approves,
and kisses are a better fate
than wisdom
lady i swear by all flowers.   Don't cry
—the best gesture of my brain is less than
your eyelids' flutter which says

we are for each other: then
laugh, leaning back in my arms
for life's not a paragraph

And death i think is no parenthesis

if i have made,my lady,intricate
imperfect various things chiefly which wrong
your eyes(frailer than most deep dreams are frail)
songs less firm than your body's whitest song
upon my mind—if i have failed to snare
the glance too shy—if through my singing slips
the very skillful strangeness of your smile
the keen primeval silence of your hair

—let the world say "his most wise music stole
nothing from death"—
                                        you only will create
(who are so perfectly alive)my shame:
lady through whose profound and fragile lips
the sweet small clumsy feet of April came

into the ragged meadow of my soul.

i sing of Olaf glad and big
whose warmest heart recoiled at war:
a conscientious object-or

his wellbelovéd colonel(trig
westpointer most succinctly bred)
took erring Olaf soon in hand;
but—though an host of overjoyed
noncoms(first knocking on the head
him)do through icy waters roll
that helplessness which others stroke
with brushes recently employed
anent this muddy toiletbowl,
while kindred intellects evoke
allegiance per blunt instruments—
Olaf(being to all intents
a corpse and wanting any rag
upon what God unto him gave)
responds,without getting annoyed
"I will not kiss your f.ing flag"

straightway the silver bird looked grave
(departing hurriedly to shave)

but—though all kinds of officers
(a yearning nation's blueeyed pride)
their passive prey did kick and curse
until for wear their clarion
voices and boots were much the worse,
and egged the firstclassprivates on
his rectum wickedly to tease
by means of skilfully applied
bayonets roasted hot with heat—
Olaf(upon what were once knees)
does almost ceaselessly repeat
"there is some s. I will not eat"

our president,being of which
assertions duly notified
threw the yellowsonofabitch
into a dungeon,where he died

Christ(of His mercy infinite)
i pray to see;and Olaf,too

preponderatingly because
unless statistics lie he was
more brave than me:more blond than you.

if there are any heavens my mother will(all by herself)have
one.   It will not be a pansy heaven nor
a fragile heaven of lilies-of-the-valley but
it will be a heaven of blackred roses

my father will be(deep like a rose
tall like a rose)

standing near my

(swaying over her
silent)
with eyes which are really petals and see

nothing with the face of a poet really which
is a flower and not a face with
hands
which whisper
This is my beloved my

                          (suddenly in sunlight
he will bow,

& the whole garden will bow)

but if a living dance upon dead minds
why,it is love;but at the earliest spear
of sun perfectly should disappear
moon's utmost magic,or stones speak or one
name control more incredible splendor than
our merely universe,love's also there:
and being here imprisoned,tortured here
love everywhere exploding maims and blinds
(but surely does not forget,perish,sleep
cannot be photographed,measured;disdains
the trivial labelling of punctual brains. . .
—Who wields a poem huger than the grave?
from only Whom shall time no refuge keep
though all the weird worlds must be opened?
)Love

may i feel said he
(i'll squeal said she
just once said he)
it's fun said she

(may i touch said he
how much said she
a lot said he)
why not said she

(let's go said he
not too far said she
what's too far said he
where you are said she)

may i stay said he
(which way said she
like this said he
if you kiss said she

may i move said he
is it love said she)
if you're willing said he
(but you're killing said she

but it's life said he
but your wife said she
now said he)
ow said she

(tiptop said he
don't stop said she
oh no said he)
go slow said she

(cccome?said he
ummm said she)
you're divine!said he
(you are Mine said she)

kumrads die because they're told)
kumrads die before they're old
(kumrads aren't afraid to die
kumrads don't
and kumrads won't
believe in life)and death knows whie

(all good kumrads you can tell
by their altruistic smell
moscow pipes good kumrads dance)
kumrads enjoy
s.freud knows whoy
the hope that you may mess your pance

every kumrad is a bit
of quite unmitigated hate
(travelling in a futile groove
god knows why)
and so do i
(because they are afraid to love

conceive a man,should he have anything
would give a little more than it away

(his autumn's winter being summer's spring
who moved by standing in november's may)
from whose(if loud most howish time derange

the silent whys of such a deathlessness)
remembrance might no patient mind unstrange
learn(nor could all earth's rotting scholars guess
that life shall not for living find the rule)

and dark beginnings are his luminous ends
who far less lonely than a fire is cool
took bedfellows for moons mountains for friends

—open your thighs to fate and(if you can
withholding nothing)World,conceive a man

what a proud dreamhorse pulling(smoothloomingly)through
(stepp)this(ing)crazily seething of this
raving city screamingly street wonderful

flowers And o the Light thrown by Them opens

sharp holes in dark places paints eyes touches hands with new-
ness and these startled whats are a(piercing clothes thoughts kiss
-ing wishes bodies)squirm-of-frightened shy are whichs small
its hungry for Is for Love Spring thirsty for happens
only and beautiful
                        there is a ragged beside the who limps
man crying silence upward
                            —to have tasted Beautiful to have known
Only to have smelled Happens—skip dance kids hop point at
red blue yellow violet white orange green-
ness

     o what a proud dreamhorse moving(whose feet
almost walk air). now who stops. Smiles.he
                                        stamps

Jehovah buried,Satan dead,
do fearers worship Much and Quick;
badness not being felt as bad,
itself thinks goodness what is meek;
obey says toc,submit says tic,
Eternity's a Five Year Plan:
if Joy with Pain shall hang in hock
who dares to call himself a man?

go dreamless knaves on Shadows fed,
your Harry's Tom,your Tom is Dick;
while Gadgets murder squawk and add,
the cult of Same is all the chic;
by instruments,both span and spic,
are justly measured Spic and Span:
to kiss the mike if Jew turn kike
who dares to call himself a man?

loudly for Truth have liars pled,
their heels for Freedom slaves will click;
where Boobs are holy,poets mad,
illustrious punks of Progress shriek;
when Souls are outlawed,Hearts are sick,
Hearts being sick,Minds nothing can:
if Hate's a game and Love's a φυκ
who dares to call himself a man?

King Christ,this world is all aleak;
and lifepreservers there are none:
and waves which only He may walk
Who dares to call Himself a man.

this mind made war
being generous
this heart could dare)
unhearts can less

unminds must fear
because and why
what filth is here
unlives do cry

on him they shat
they shat encore
he laughed and spat
(this life could dare

freely to give
as gives a friend
not those who slave
unselves to lend

for hope of hope
must coo or boo
may strut or creep
ungenerous who

ape deftly aims
they dare not share)
such make their names
(this poet made war

whose naught and all
sun are and moon
come fair come foul
he goes alone

daring to dare
for joy of joy)
what stink is here
unpoets do cry

unfools unfree
undeaths who live
nor shall they be
and must they have

at him they fart
they fart full oft
(with mind with heart
he spat and laughed

with self with life
this poet arose
nor hate nor grief
can go where goes

this whyless soul
a loneliest road
who dares to stroll
almost this god

this surely dream
perhaps this ghost)
humbly and whom
for worst or best

(and proudly things
only which grow
and the rain's wings
the birds of snow

things without name
beyond because
things over blame
things under praise

glad things or free
truly which live
always shall be
may never have)

do i salute
(by moon by sun
i deeply greet
this fool and man

love's function is to fabricate unknownness

(known being wishless;but love,all of wishing)
though life's lived wrongsideout,sameness chokes oneness
truth is confused with fact,fish boast of fishing

and men are caught by worms(love may not care
if time totters,light droops,all measures bend
nor marvel if a thought should weigh a star
—dreads dying least;and less,that death should end)

how lucky lovers are(whose selves abide
under whatever shall discovered be)
whose ignorant each breathing dares to hide
more than most fabulous wisdom fears to see

(who laugh and cry)who dream,create and kill
while the whole moves;and every part stands still:

death(having lost)put on his universe
and yawned:it looks like rain
(they've played for timelessness
with chips of when)
that's yours;i guess
you'll have to loan me pain
to take the hearse,
see you again.

Love(having found)wound up such pretty toys
as themselves could not know:
the earth tinily whirls;
while daisies grow
(and boys and girls
have whispered thus and so)
and girls with boys
to bed will go,

(of Ever-Ever Land i speak
sweet morons gather roun'
who does not dare to stand or sit
may take it lying down)

down with the human soul
and anything else uncanned
for everyone carries canopeners
in Ever-Ever Land

(for Ever-Ever Land is a place
that's as simple as simple can be
and was built that way on purpose
by simple people like we)

down with hell and heaven
and all the religious fuss
infinity pleased our parents
one inch looks good to us

(and Ever-Ever Land is a place
that's measured and safe and known
where it's lucky to be unlucky
and the hitler lies down with the cohn)

down above all with love
and everything perverse
or which makes some feel more better
when all ought to feel less worse

(but only sameness is normal
in Ever-Ever Land
for a bad cigar is a woman
but a gland is only a gland)

my specialty is living said
a man(who could not earn his bread
because he would not sell his head)

squads right impatiently replied
two billion pubic lice inside
one pair of trousers(which had died)

if i

or anybody don't
know where it her his

my next meal's çoming from
i say to hell with that
that doesn't matter(and if

he she it or everybody gets a
bellyful without
lifting my finger i say to hell
with that i

say that doesn't matter)but
if somebody
or you are beautiful or
deep or generous what
i say is

whistle that
sing that yell that spell
that out big(bigger than cosmic
rays war earthquakes famine or the ex

prince of whoses diving into
a whatses to rescue miss nobody's
probably handbag)because i say that's not

swell(get me)babe not(understand me)lousy
kid that's something else my sweet(i feel that's

true)

may my heart always be open to little
birds who are the secrets of living
whatever they sing is better than to know
and if men should not hear them men are old

may my mind stroll about hungry
and fearless and thirsty and supple
and even if it's sunday may i be wrong
for whenever men are right they are not young

and may myself do nothing usefully
and love yourself so more than truly
there's never been quite such a fool who could fail
pulling all the sky over him with one smile

you shall above all things be glad and young.
For if you're young,whatever life you wear

it will become you;and if you are glad
whatever's living will yourself become.
Girlboys may nothing more than boygirls need:
i can entirely her only love

whose any mystery makes every man's
flesh put space on;and his mind take off time

that you should ever think,may god forbid
and(in his mercy)your true lover spare:
for that way knowledge lies,the foetal grave
called progress,and negation's dead undoom.

I'd rather learn from one bird how to sing
than teach ten thousand stars how not to dance

flotsam and jetsam
are gentlemen poeds
urseappeal netsam
our spinsters and coeds)

thoroughly bretish
they scout the inhuman
itarian fetish
that man isn't wuman

vive the millenni
um three cheers for labor
give all things to enni
one bugger thy nabor

(neck and senecktie
are gentlemen ppoyds
even whose recktie
are covered by lloyd's

red-rag and pink-flag
blackshirt and brown
strut-mince and stink-brag
have all come to town

some like it shot
and some like it hung
and some like it in the twot
nine months young

as freedom is a breakfastfood
or truth can live with right and wrong
or molehills are from mountains made
—long enough and just so long
will being pay the rent of seem
and genius please the talentgang
and water most encourage flame

as hatracks into peachtrees grow
or hopes dance best on bald men's hair
and every finger is a toe
and any courage is a fear
—long enough and just so long
will the impure think all things pure
and hornets wail by children stung

or as the seeing are the blind
and robins never welcome spring
nor flatfolk prove their world is round
nor dingsters die at break of dong
and common's rare and millstones float
—long enough and just so long
tomorrow will not be too late

worms are the words but joy's the voice
down shall go which and up come who
breasts will be breasts thighs will be thighs
deeds cannot dream what dreams can do
—time is a tree(this life one leaf)
but love is the sky and i am for you
just so long and long enough

anyone lived in a pretty how town
(with up so floating many bells down)
spring summer autumn winter
he sang his didn't he danced his did.

Women and men(both little and small)
cared for anyone not at all
they sowed their isn't they reaped their same
sun moon stars rain

children guessed(but only a few
and down they forgot as up they grew
autumn winter spring summer)
that noone loved him more by more

when by now and tree by leaf
she laughed his joy she cried his grief
bird by snow and stir by still
anyone's any was all to her

someones married their everyones
laughed their cryings and did their dance
(sleep wake hope and then)they
said their nevers they slept their dream

stars rain sun moon
(and only the snow can begin to explain
how children are apt to forget to remember
with up so floating many bells down)

one day anyone died i guess
(and noone stooped to kiss his face)
busy folk buried them side by side
little by little and was by was

all by all and deep by deep
and more by more they dream their sleep
noone and anyone earth by april
wish by spirit and if by yes.

Women and men(both dong and ding)
summer autumn winter spring
reaped their sowing and went their came
sun moon stars rain

my father moved through dooms of love
through sames of am through haves of give,
singing each morning out of each night
my father moved through depths of height

this motionless forgetful where
turned at his glance to shining here;
that if(so timid air is firm)
under his eyes would stir and squirm

newly as from unburied which
floats the first who,his april touch
drove sleeping selves to swarm their fates
woke dreamers to their ghostly roots

and should some why completely weep
my father's fingers brought her sleep:
vainly no smallest voice might cry
for he could feel the mountains grow.

Lifting the valleys of the sea
my father moved through griefs of joy;
praising a forehead called the moon
singing desire into begin

joy was his song and joy so pure
a heart of star by him could steer
and pure so now and now so yes
the wrists of twilight would rejoice

keen as midsummer's keen beyond
conceiving mind of sun will stand,
so strictly(over utmost him
so hugely)stood my father's dream

his flesh was flesh his blood was blood:
no hungry man but wished him food;
no cripple wouldn't creep one mile
uphill to only see him smile.

Scorning the pomp of must and shall
my father moved through dooms of feel;
his anger was as right as rain
his pity was as green as grain

septembering arms of year extend
less humbly wealth to foe and friend
than he to foolish and to wise
offered immeasurable is

proudly and(by octobering flame
beckoned)as earth will downward climb,
so naked for immortal work
his shoulders marched against the dark

his sorrow was as true as bread:
no liar looked him in the head;
if every friend became his foe
he'd laugh and build a world with snow.

My father moved through theys of we,
singing each new leaf out of each tree
(and every child was sure that spring
danced when she heard my father sing)

then let men kill which cannot share,
let blood and flesh be mud and mire,
scheming imagine,passion willed,
freedom a drug that's bought and sold

giving to steal and cruel kind,
a heart to fear,to doubt a mind,
to differ a disease of same,
conform the pinnacle of am

though dull were all we taste as bright,
bitter all utterly things sweet,
maggoty minus and dumb death
all we inherit,all bequeath

and nothing quite so least as truth
—i say though hate were why men breathe—
because my father lived his soul
love is the whole and more than all

i say no world

can hold a you
shall see the not
because
and why but
(who
stood within his steam be-
ginning and
began to sing all
here is hands machine no

good too quick i know this
suit you pay
a store too
much yes what
too much o much cheap
me i work i know i say i have
not any
never
no vacation here

is hands is work since i am
born is good
but there this cheap this suit too
quick no suit there every
-thing
nothing i
say the
world not fit
you)he is

not(i say the world
yes any world is much
too not quite big enough to
hold one tiny this with
time's
more than
most how
immeasurable
anguish

pregnant one fearless
one good yes
completely kind
mindheart one true one generous child-
man
-god one eager
souldoll one
unsellable not buyable alive
one i say human being)one

goldberger

these children singing in stone a
silence of stone these
little children wound with stone
flowers opening for

ever these silently lit
tle children are petals
their song is a flower of
always their flowers

of stone are
silently singing
a song more silent
than silence these always

children forever
singing wreathed with singing
blossoms children of
stone with blossoming

eyes
know if a
lit tle
tree listens

forever to always children singing forever
a song made
of silent as stone silence of
song

love is more thicker than forget
more thinner than recall
more seldom than a wave is wet
more frequent than to fail

it is most mad and moonly
and less it shall unbe
than all the sea which only
is deeper than the sea

love is less always than to win
less never than alive
less bigger than the least begin
less littler than forgive

it is most sane and sunly
and more it cannot die
than all the sky which only
is higher than the sky

hate blows a bubble of despair into
hugeness world system universe and bang
—fear buries a tomorrow under woe
and up comes yesterday most green and young

pleasure and pain are merely surfaces
(one itself showing,itself hiding one)
life's only and true value neither is
love makes the little thickness of the coin

comes here a man would have from madame death
neverless now and without winter spring?
she'll spin that spirit her own fingers with
and give him nothing(if he should not sing)

how much more than enough for both of us
darling.   And if i sing you are my voice,

what freedom's not some under's mere above
but breathing yes which fear will never no?
measureless our pure living complete love
whose doom is beauty and its fate to grow

shall hate confound the wise?doubt blind the brave?
does mask wear face?have singings gone to say?
here youngest selves yet younger selves conceive
here's music's music and the day of day

are worlds collapsing?any was a glove
but i'm and you are actual either hand
is when for sale?forever is to give
and on forever's very now we stand

nor a first rose explodes but shall increase
whole truthful infinite immediate us

of all the blessings which to man
kind progress doth impart
one stands supreme i mean the an
imal without a heart.

Huge this collective pseudobeast
(sans either pain or joy)
does nothing except preexist
its hoi in its polloi

and if sometimes he's prodded forth
to exercise her vote
(or made by threats of something worth
than death to change their coat

—which something as you'll never guess
in fifty thousand years
equals the quote and unquote loss
of liberty my dears—

or even is compelled to fight
itself from tame to teem)
still doth our hero contemplate
in raptures of undream

that strictly(and how)scienti
fic land of supernod
where freedom is compulsory
and only man is god.

Without a heart the animal
is very very kind
so kind it wouldn't like a soul
and couldn't use a mind

ygUDuh

    ydoan
    yunnuhstaɳ

    ydoan o
    yunnuhstan dem
    yguduh ged

    yunnuhstan dem doidee
    yguduh ged riduh
    ydoan o nudn
LISN bud LISN

        dem
        gud
        am

        lidl yelluh bas
        tuds weer goin

duhSIVILEYEzum

a salesman is an it that stinks Excuse

Me whether it's president of the you were say
or a jennelman name misder finger isn't
important whether it's millions of other punks
or just a handful absolutely doesn't
matter and whether it's in lonjewray

or shrouds is immaterial it stinks

a salesman is an it that stinks to please

but whether to please itself or someone else
makes no more difference than if it sells
hate condoms education snakeoil vac
uumcleaners terror strawberries democ
ra(caveat emptor)cy superfluous hair

or Think We've Met subhuman rights Before

a politician is an arse upon
which everyone has sat except a man

plato told

him:he couldn't
believe it(jesus

told him;he
wouldn't believe
it)lao

tsze
certainly told
him,and general
(yes

mam)
sherman;
and even
(believe it
or

not)you
told him:i told
him;we told him
(he didn't believe it,no

sir)it took
a nipponized bit of
the old sixth

avenue
el;in the top of his head:to tell

him

pity this busy monster,manunkind,

not.   Progress is a comfortable disease:
your victim(death and life safely beyond)

plays with the bigness of his littleness
—electrons deify one razorblade
into a mountainrange;lenses extend

unwish through curving wherewhen till unwish
returns on its unself.
                    A world of made
is not a world of born—pity poor flesh

and trees,poor stars and stones,but never this
fine specimen of hypermagical

ultraomnipotence.   We doctors know

a hopeless case if—listen:there's a hell
of a good universe next door;let's go

one's not half two.   It's two are halves of one:
which halves reintegrating,shall occur
no death and any quantity;but than
all numerable mosts the actual more

minds ignorant of stern miraculous
this every truth—beware of heartless them
(given the scalpel,they dissect a kiss;
or,sold the reason,they undream a dream)

one is the song which fiends and angels sing:
all murdering lies by mortals told make two.
Let liars wilt,repaying life they're loaned;
we(by a gift called dying born)must grow

deep in dark least ourselves remembering
love only rides his year.
                                    All lose,whole find

what if a much of a which of a wind
gives the truth to summer's lie;
bloodies with dizzying leaves the sun
and yanks immortal stars awry?
Blow king to beggar and queen to seem
(blow friend to fiend:blow space to time)
—when skies are hanged and oceans drowned,
the single secret will still be man

what if a keen of a lean wind flays
screaming hills with sleet and snow:
strangles valleys by ropes of thing
and stifles forests in white ago?
Blow hope to terror;blow seeing to blind
(blow pity to envy and soul to mind)
—whose hearts are mountains,roots are trees,
it's they shall cry hello to the spring

what if a dawn of a doom of a dream
bites this universe in two,
peels forever out of his grave
and sprinkles nowhere with me and you?
Blow soon to never and never to twice
(blow life to isn't:blow death to was)
—all nothing's only our hugest home;
the most who die,the more we live

no man,if men are gods;but if gods must
be men,the sometimes only man is this
(most common,for each anguish is his grief;
and,for his joy is more than joy,most rare)

a fiend,if fiends speak truth;if angels burn

by their own generous completely light,
an angel;or(as various worlds he'll spurn
rather than fail immeasurable fate)
coward,clown,traitor,idiot,dreamer,beast—

such was a poet and shall be and is

—who'll solve the depths of horror to defend
a sunbeam's architecture with his life:
and carve immortal jungles of despair
to hold a mountain's heartbeat in his hand

when god decided to invent
everything he took one
breath bigger than a circustent
and everything began

when man determined to destroy
himself he picked the was
of shall and finding only why
smashed it into because

rain or hail
sam done
the best he kin
till they digged his hole

:sam was a man

stout as a bridge
rugged as a bear
slickern a weazel
how be you

(sun or snow)

gone into what
like all them kings
you read about
and on him sings

a whippoorwill;

heart was big
as the world aint square
with room for the devil
and his angels too

yes,sir

what may be better
or what may be worse
and what may be clover
clover clover

(nobody'll know)

sam was a man
grinned his grin
done his chores
laid him down.

Sleep well

nothing false and possible is love
(who's imagined,therefore limitless)
love's to giving as to keeping's give;
as yes is to if,love is to yes

must's a schoolroom in the month of may:
life's the deathboard where all now turns when
(love's a universe beyond obey
or command,reality or un-)

proudly depths above why's first because
(faith's last doubt and humbly heights below)
kneeling,we—true lovers—pray that us
will ourselves continue to outgrow

all whose mosts if you have known and i've
only we our least begin to guess

true lovers in each happening of their hearts
live longer than all which and every who;
despite what fear denies,what hope asserts,
what falsest both disprove by proving true

(all doubts,all certainties,as villains strive
and heroes through the mere mind's poor pretend
—grim comics of duration:only love
immortally occurs beyond the mind)

such a forever is love's any now
and her each here is such an everywhere,
even more true would truest lovers grow
if out of midnight dropped more suns than are

(yes;and if time should ask into his was
all shall,their eyes would never miss a yes)

yes is a pleasant country:
if's wintry
(my lovely)
let's open the year

both is the very weather
(not either)
my treasure,
when violets appear

love is a deeper season
than reason;
my sweet one
(and april's where we're)

all ignorance toboggans into know
and trudges up to ignorance again:
but winter's not forever,even snow
melts;and if spring should spoil the game,what then?

all history's a winter sport or three:
but were it five,i'd still insist that all
history is too small for even me;
for me and you,exceedingly too small.

Swoop(shrill collective myth)into thy grave
merely to toil the scale to shrillerness
per every madge and mabel dick and dave
—tomorrow is our permanent address

and there they'll scarcely find us(if they do,
we'll move away still further:into now

darling!because my blood can sing
and dance(and does with each your least
your any most very amazing now
or here)let pitiless fear play host
to every isn't that's under the spring
—but if a look should april me,
down isn't's own isn't go ghostly they

doubting can turn men's see to stare
their faith to how their joy to why
their stride and breathing to limp and prove
—but if a look should april me,
some thousand million hundred more
bright worlds than merely by doubting have
darkly themselves unmade makes love

armies(than hate itself and no
meanness unsmaller)armies can
immensely meet for centuries
and(except nothing)nothing's won
—but if a look should april me
for half a when,whatever is less
alive than never begins to yes

but if a look should april me
(though such as perfect hope can feel
only despair completely strikes
forests of mind,mountains of soul)
quite at the hugest which of his who
death is killed dead.   Hills jump with brooks:
trees tumble out of twigs and sticks;

"sweet spring is your
time is my time is our
time for springtime is lovetime
and viva sweet love"

(all the merry little birds are
flying in the floating in the
very spirits singing in
are winging in the blossoming)

lovers go and lovers come
awandering awondering
but any two are perfectly
alone there's nobody else alive

(such a sky and such a sun
i never knew and neither did you
and everybody never breathed
quite so many kinds of yes)

not a tree can count his leaves
each herself by opening
but shining who by thousands mean
only one amazing thing

(secretly adoring shyly
tiny winging darting floating
merry in the blossoming
always joyful selves are singing)

"sweet spring is your
time is my time is our
time for springtime is lovetime
and viva sweet love"

o by the by
has anybody seen
little you-i
who stood on a green
hill and threw
his wish at blue

with a swoop and a dart
out flew his wish
(it dived like a fish
but it climbed like a dream)
throbbing like a heart
singing like a flame

blue took it my
far beyond far
and high beyond high
bluer took it your
but bluest took it our
away beyond where

what a wonderful thing
is the end of a string
(murmurs little you-i
as the hill becomes nil)
and will somebody tell
me why people let go

if everything happens that can't be done
(and anything's righter
than books
could plan)
the stupidest teacher will almost guess
(with a run
skip
around we go yes)
there's nothing as something as one

one hasn't a why or because or although
(and buds know better
than books
don't grow)
one's anything old being everything new
(with a what
which
around we come who)
one's everyanything so

so world is a leaf so tree is a bough
(and birds sing sweeter
than books
tell how)
so here is away and so your is a my
(with a down
up
around again fly)
forever was never till now

now i love you and you love me
(and books are shuter
than books
can be)
and deep in the high that does nothing but fall
(with a shout
each
around we go all)
there's somebody calling who's we

we're anything brighter than even the sun
(we're everything greater
than books
might mean)
we're everyanything more than believe
(with a spin
leap
alive we're alive)
we're wonderful one times one

when serpents bargain for the right to squirm
and the sun strikes to gain a living wage—
when thorns regard their roses with alarm
and rainbows are insured against old age

when every thrush may sing no new moon in
if all screech-owls have not okayed his voice
—and any wave signs on the dotted line
or else an ocean is compelled to close

when the oak begs permission of the birch
to make an acorn—valleys accuse their
mountains of having altitude—and march
denounces april as a saboteur

then we'll believe in that incredible
unanimal mankind(and not until)

o to be in finland
now that russia's here)

swing low
sweet ca

rr
y on

(pass the freedoms pappy or
uncle shylock not interested

no time ago
or else a life
walking in the dark
i met christ

jesus)my heart
flopped over
and lay still
while he passed(as

close as i'm to you
yes closer
made of nothing
except loneliness

who were so dark of heart they might not speak,
a little innocence will make them sing;
teach them to see who could not learn to look
—from the reality of all nothing

will actually lift a luminous whole;
turn sheer despairing to most perfect gay,
nowhere to here,never to beautiful:
a little innocence creates a day.

And something thought or done or wished without
a little innocence,although it were
as red as terror and as green as fate,
greyly shall fail and dully disappear—

but the proud power of himself death immense
is not so as a little innocence

to start,to hesitate;to stop
(kneeling in doubt:while all
skies fall)and then to slowly trust
T upon H,and smile

could anything be pleasanter
(some big dark little day
which seems a lifetime at the least)
except to add an A?

henceforth he feels his pride involved
(this i who's also you)
and nothing less than excellent
E will exactly do

next(our great problem nearly solved)
we dare adorn the whole
with a distinct grandiloquent
deep D;while all skies fall

at last perfection,now and here
—but look:not sunlight?yes!
and(plunging rapturously up)
we spill our masterpiece

if(touched by love's own secret)we, like homing
through welcoming sweet miracles of air
(and joyfully all truths of wing resuming)
selves,into infinite tomorrow steer

—souls under whom flow(mountain valley forest)
a million wheres which never may become
one(wholly strange;familiar wholly)dearest
more than reality of more than dream—

how should contented fools of fact envision
the mystery of freedom?yet,among
their loud exactitudes of imprecision,
you'll(silently alighting)and i'll sing

while at us very deafly a most stares
colossal hoax of clocks and calendars

i thank You God for most this amazing
day:for the leaping greenly spirits of trees
and a blue true dream of sky;and for everything
which is natural which is infinite which is yes

(i who have died am alive again today,
and this is the sun's birthday;this is the birth
day of life and of love and wings:and of the gay
great happening illimitably earth)

how should tasting touching hearing seeing
breathing any—lifted from the no
of all nothing—human merely being
doubt unimaginable You?

(now the ears of my ears awake and
now the eyes of my eyes are opened)

the great advantage of being alive
(instead of undying)is not so much
that mind no more can disprove than prove
what heart may feel and soul may touch
—the great(my darling)happens to be
that love are in we,that love are in we

and here is a secret they never will share
for whom create is less than have
or one times one than when times where—
that we are in love,that we are in love:
with us they've nothing times nothing to do
(for love are in we am in i are in you)

this world(as timorous itsters all
to call their cowardice quite agree)
shall never discover our touch and feel
—for love are in we are in love are in we;
for you are and i am and we are(above
and under all possible worlds)in love

a billion brains may coax undeath
from fancied fact and spaceful time—
no heart can leap,no soul can breathe
but by the sizeless truth of a dream
whose sleep is the sky and the earth and the sea.
For love are in you am in i are in we

when faces called flowers float out of the ground
and breathing is wishing and wishing is having—
but keeping is downward and doubting and never
—it's april(yes,april;my darling)it's spring!
yes the pretty birds frolic as spry as can fly
yes the little fish gambol as glad as can be
(yes the mountains are dancing together)

when every leaf opens without any sound
and wishing is having and having is giving—
but keeping is doting and nothing and nonsense
—alive;we're alive,dear:it's(kiss me now)spring!
now the pretty birds hover so she and so he
now the little fish quiver so you and so i
(now the mountains are dancing,the mountains)

when more than was lost has been found has been found
and having is giving and giving is living—
but keeping is darkness and winter and cringing
—it's spring(all our night becomes day)o,it's spring!
all the pretty birds dive to the heart of the sky
all the little fish climb through the mind of the sea
(all the mountains are dancing;are dancing)

now all the fingers of this tree(darling)have
hands,and all the hands have people;and
more each particular person is(my love)
alive than every world can understand

and now you are and i am now and we're
a mystery which will never happen again,
a miracle which has never happened before—
and shining this our now must come to then

our then shall be some darkness during which
fingers are without hands;and i have no
you:and all trees are(any more than each
leafless)its silent in forevering snow

—but never fear(my own,my beautiful
my blossoming)for also then's until

luminous tendril of celestial wish

(whying diminutive bright deathlessness
to these my not themselves believing eyes
adventuring,enormous nowhere from)

querying affirmation;virginal

immediacy of precision:more
and perfectly more most ethereal
silence through twilight's mystery made flesh—

dreamslender exquisite white firstful flame

—new moon!as(by the miracle of your
sweet innocence refuted)clumsy some
dull cowardice called a world vanishes,

teach disappearing also me the keen
illimitable secret of begin

maggie and milly and molly and may
went down to the beach(to play one day)

and maggie discovered a shell that sang
so sweetly she couldn't remember her troubles,and

milly befriended a stranded star
whose rays five languid fingers were;

and molly was chased by a horrible thing
which raced sideways while blowing bubbles:and

may came home with a smooth round stone
as small as a world and as large as alone.

For whatever we lose(like a you or a me)
it's always ourselves we find in the sea

in time's a noble mercy of proportion
with generosities beyond believing
(though flesh and blood accuse him of coercion
or mind and soul convict him of deceiving)

whose ways are neither reasoned nor unreasoned,
his wisdom cancels conflict and agreement
—saharas have their centuries;ten thousand
of which are smaller than a rose's moment

there's time for laughing and there's time for crying—
for hoping for despair for peace for longing
—a time for growing and a time for dying:
a night for silence and a day for singing

but more than all(as all your more than eyes
tell me)there is a time for timelessness

So shy shy shy(and with a
look the very boldest man
can scarcely dare to meet no matter

how he'll try to try)

So wrong(wrong wrong)and with a
smile at which the rightest man
remembers there is such a thing

as spring and wonders why

So gay gay gay and with a
wisdom not the wisest man
will partly understand(although

the wisest man am i)

So young young young and with a
something makes the oldest man
(whoever he may be)the only

man who'll never die

in time of daffodils(who know
the goal of living is to grow)
forgetting why,remember how

in time of lilacs who proclaim
the aim of waking is to dream,
remember so(forgetting seem)

in time of roses(who amaze
our now and here with paradise)
forgetting if,remember yes

in time of all sweet things beyond
whatever mind may comprehend,
remember seek(forgetting find)

and in a mystery to be
(when time from time shall set us free)
forgetting me,remember me

that melancholy

fellow'll play
his handorgan
until you say

"i want a fortune"

.At which(smiling)he stops:
& pick
ing up a magical stick
t,a,p,s

this dingy cage:then with a ghost

's rainfaint windthin
voice-which-is
no-voice sobcries

"paw?lee"

—whereupon out(SlO
wLy)steps(to
mount the wand)a by no
means almost

white morethanPerson;who

(riding through space
to diminutive this
opened drawer)tweak

S with his brutebeak

one fatal faded(pinkish or
yellowish maybe)piece
of pitiful paper—
but now,as Mr bowing Cockatoo

proffers the meaning of the stars

14th st dis(because my tears
are full of eyes)appears.   Because
only the truest things always

are true because they can't be true

THANKSGIVING
(1956)

a monstering horror swallows
this unworld me by you
as the god of our fathers' fathers bows
to a which that walks like a who

but the voice-with-a-smile of democracy
announces night & day
"all poor little peoples that want to be free
just trust in the u s a"

suddenly uprose hungary
and she gave a terrible cry
"no slave's unlife shall murder me
for i will freely die"

she cried so high thermopylae
heard her and marathon
and all prehuman history
and finally The UN

"be quiet little hungary
and do as you are bid
a good kind bear is angry
we fear for the quo pro quid"

uncle sam shrugs his pretty
pink shoulders you know how
and he twitches a liberal titty
and lisps "i'm busy right now"

so rah-rah-rah democracy
let's all be as thankful as hell
and bury the statue of liberty
(because it begins to smell)

from spiralling ecstatically this

proud nowhere of earth's most prodigious night
blossoms a newborn babe:around him,eyes
—gifted with every keener appetite
than mere unmiracle can quite appease—
humbly in their imagined bodies kneel
(over time space doom dream while floats the whole

perhapsless mystery of paradise)

mind without soul may blast some universe
to might have been,and stop ten thousand stars
but not one heartbeat of this child;nor shall
even prevail a million questionings
against the silence of his mother's smile

—whose only secret all creation sings

out of the lie of no
rises a truth of yes
(only herself and who
illimitably is)

making fools understand
(like wintry me)that not
all matterings of mind
equal one violet

whatever's merely wilful,
and not miraculous
(be never it so skilful)
must wither fail and cease
—but better than to grow
beauty knows no

their goal(in calm and fury:
through joy and anguish)who've
made her,outglory glory
the little while they live—
unless by your thinking
forever's long

let beauty touch a blunder
(called life)we die to breathe,
itself becomes her wonder
—and wonderful is death;
but more,the older he's
the younger she's

stand with your lover on the ending earth—

and while a(huge which by which huger than
huge)whoing sea leaps to greenly hurl snow

suppose we could not love,dear;imagine

ourselves like living neither nor dead these
(or many thousand hearts which don't and dream
or many million minds which sleep and move)
blind sands,at pitiless the mercy of

time time time time time

—how fortunate are you and i,whose home
is timelessness:we who have wandered down
from fragrant mountains of eternal now

to frolic in such mysteries as birth
and death a day(or maybe even less)

i am a little church(no great cathedral)
far from the splendor and squalor of hurrying cities
—i do not worry if briefer days grow briefest,
i am not sorry when sun and rain make april

my life is the life of the reaper and the sower;
my prayers are prayers of earth's own clumsily striving
(finding and losing and laughing and crying)children
whose any sadness or joy is my grief or my gladness

around me surges a miracle of unceasing
birth and glory and death and resurrection:
over my sleeping self float flaming symbols
of hope,and i wake to a perfect patience of mountains

i am a little church(far from the frantic
world with its rapture and anguish)at peace with nature
—i do not worry if longer nights grow longest;
i am not sorry when silence becomes singing

winter by spring,i lift my diminutive spire to
merciful Him Whose only now is forever:
standing erect in the deathless truth of His presence
(welcoming humbly His light and proudly His darkness)

all nearness pauses,while a star can grow

all distance breathes a final dream of bells;
perfectly outlined against afterglow
are all amazing the and peaceful hills

(not where not here but neither's blue most both)

and history immeasurably is
wealthier by a single sweet day's death:
as not imagined secrecies comprise

goldenly huge whole the upfloating moon.

Time's a strange fellow;
                          more he gives than takes
(and he takes all)nor any marvel finds
quite disappearance but some keener makes
losing,gaining
                —love!if a world ends

more than all worlds begin to(see?)begin

how generous is that himself the sun

—arriving truly,faithfully who goes
(never a moment ceasing to begin
the mystery of day for someone's eyes)

with silver splendors past conceiving who

comforts his children,if he disappears;
till of more much than dark most nowhere no
particle is not a universe—

but if,with goldenly his fathering

(as that himself out of all silence strolls)
nearness awakened,any bird should sing:
and our night's thousand million miracles

a million thousand hundred nothings seem
—we are himself's own self;his very him

joyful your complete fearless and pure love
with one least ignorance may comprehend
more than shall ever provingly disprove
eithering vastnesses of orish mind

—nothing believable inhabits here:
overs of known descend through depths of guess,
shadows are substances and wings are birds;
unders of dream adventure truths of skies—

darling of darlings!by that miracle
which is the coming of pure joyful your
fearless and complete love,all safely small
big wickedly worlds of world disappear

all and(like any these my)words of words
turn to a silence who's the voice of voice

rosetree,rosetree
—you're a song to see:whose
all(you're a sight to sing)
poems are opening,
as if an earth was
playing at birthdays

each(a wish no
bigger than)in roguish
am of fragrance
dances a honeydunce;
whirling's a frantic
struts a pedantic

proud or humble,
equally they're welcome
—as if the humble proud
youngest bud testified
"giving(and giving
only)is living"

worlds of prose mind
utterly beyond is
brief that how infinite
(deeply immediate
fleet and profound this)
beautiful kindness

sweet such(past can's
every can't)immensest
mysteries contradict
a deathful realm of fact
—by their precision
evolving vision

dreamtree,truthtree
tree of jubilee:with
aeons of(trivial
merely)existence,all
when may not measure
a now of your treasure

blithe each shameless
gaiety of blossom
—blissfully nonchalant
wise and each ignorant
gladness—unteaches
what despair preaches

myriad wonder
people of a person;
joyful your any new
(every more only you)
most emanation
creates creation

lovetree!least the
rose alive must three,must
four and(to quite become
nothing)five times,proclaim
fate isn't fatal
—a heart her each petal

unlove's the heavenless hell and homeless home

of knowledgeable shadows(quick to seize
each nothing which all soulless wraiths proclaim
substance;all heartless spectres,happiness)

lovers alone wear sunlight. The whole truth

not hid by matter;not by mind revealed
(more than all dying life,all living death)
and never which has been or will be told

sings only—and all lovers are the song.

Here(only here)is freedom:always here
no then of winter equals now of spring;
but april's day transcends november's year

(eternity being so sans until
twice i have lived forever in a smile)

i carry your heart with me(i carry it in
my heart)i am never without it(anywhere
i go you go,my dear;and whatever is done
by only me is your doing,my darling)
                                        i fear
no fate(for you are my fate,my sweet)i want
no world(for beautiful you are my world,my true)
and it's you are whatever a moon has always meant
and whatever a sun will always sing is you

here is the deepest secret nobody knows
(here is the root of the root and the bud of the bud
and the sky of the sky of a tree called life;which grows
higher than soul can hope or mind can hide)
and this is the wonder that's keeping the stars apart

i carry your heart(i carry it in my heart)

spring!may—
everywhere's here
(with a low high low
and the bird on the bough)
how?why
—we never we know
(so kiss me)shy sweet eagerly my
most dear

(die!live)
the new is the true
and to lose is to have
—we never we know—
brave!brave
(the earth and the sky
are one today)my very so gay
young love

why?how—
we never we know
(with a high low high
in the may in the spring)
live!die
(forever is now)
and dance you suddenly blossoming tree
—i'll sing

being to timelessness as it's to time,
love did no more begin than love will end;
where nothing is to breathe to stroll to swim
love is the air the ocean and the land

(do lovers suffer?all divinities
proudly descending put on deathful flesh:
are lovers glad?only their smallest joy's
a universe emerging from a wish)

love is the voice under all silences,
the hope which has no opposite in fear;
the strength so strong mere force is feebleness:
the truth more first than sun more last than star

—do lovers love?why then to heaven with hell.
Whatever sages say and fools,all's well

if up's the word;and a world grows greener
minute by second and most by more—
if death is the loser and life is the winner
(and beggars are rich but misers are poor)
—let's touch the sky:
                        with a to and a fro
(and a here there where)and away we go

in even the laziest creature among us
a wisdom no knowledge can kill is astir—
now dull eyes are keen and now keen eyes are keener
(for young is the year,for young is the year)
—let's touch the sky:
                        with a great(and a gay
and a steep)deep rush through amazing day

it's brains without hearts have set saint against sinner;
put gain over gladness and joy under care—
let's do as an earth which can never do wrong does
(minute by second and most by more)
—let's touch the sky:
                        with a strange(and a true)
and a climbing fall into far near blue

if beggars are rich(and a robin will sing his
robin a song)but misers are poor—
let's love until noone could quite be(and young is
the year,dear)as living as i'm and as you're
—let's touch the sky:
                        with a you and a me
and an every(who's any who's some)one who's we

INDEX OF FIRST LINES